THE SEVEN PAGODAS

THE SEVEN PAGODAS

BY

J. W. COOMBES, B.A., A.M.S.T.

WITH 81 ILLUSTRATIONS AND A MAP

GYAN

Published by

GYAN

Gyan Publishing House
5, Ansari Road
Daryaganj, New Delhi-110002
Phone: 011-47034999, 9811692060
E-mail: books@gyanbooks.com

Distribution Network
gyanbooks.com
India, USA, Canada, UK, Australia, France

ISBN : 978-81-212-3999-8 (PB)
First Published, 1914

2nd Impression 2021

Printed at: Gyan Press, Delhi.

The Seven Pagodas
Author: J. W. Coombes

THE SEVEN PAGODAS

BY

J. W. COOMBES, B.A., A.M.S.T.

WITH 81 ILLUSTRATIONS & A MAP

LONDON

SEELEY, SERVICE & CO. LIMITED

38 GREAT RUSSELL STREET

1914

Pidariamman Ratha.

PREFACE

THIS handy guide-book is intended to help visitors whose time is limited to obtain an intelligent idea of those monuments of Hindu antiquity called by Europeans "The Seven Pagodas." Free use has been made of comments and criticisms from well-known authors on the subject, but theories of an unsatisfactory nature have been excluded. Everything worth seeing has its position marked on a map to prevent loss of time in getting about from place to place, and it would be well if they were visited in the order given.

People from all parts of the world visit the remains of these ancient sculptures, and the author will have served his special purpose in writing this short guide if the citizens of Madras, who put off seeing the place from year to year because it is so near, can be induced to hasten their visit and thereby learn something about Buddhist Hindu art which was contemporary with the early schools of ideal painting in China and Japan.

The following works have been consulted:—

"Hindu Mythology," by Wilkins; "The Ideals of Indian Art," by Havell; "The Seven Pagodas," by Carr; Fergusson's works on "Eastern Architecture" and "The Rock-Cut Temples of India"; the "Manual of the Chingleput District"; Sewell's "Antiquities"; and the "Archæological Report for 1906-7."

CONTENTS

APPENDIX

VI.—Modern Hindu Religion—*Continued.*

LIST OF ILLUSTRATIONS

SUPPLEMENTAL LIST OF ILLUSTRATIONS

FROM MESSRS. WIELE AND KLEIN, MADRAS.

FROM MISS LLOYD OF KODAIKANAL.

PHOTOGRAPHS SUPPLIED BY MADRAS ARCHÆOLOGICAL DEPARTMENT.

THE SEVEN PAGODAS

INTRODUCTION

MARCO POLO states that an arrow intended for a peacock glanced off and killed St. Thomas, the incident happening near St. Thomas's Mount, to the south of Madras. The fact is that St. Thomas was pursued and killed by his enemies, and not accidentally shot. The manner of his death is perhaps not so much a matter of interest as the allusion to his connection with the Far East, for did not the conquests of Alexander the Great afford facilities for the spread of the Gospel? India, therefore, and the East Coast were known to the merchants, and through them to the peoples around the Mediterranean basin at its Asiatic end. The south-west and north-east monsoons facilitated the progress of navigation, and the ancient port of Mahabalipuram may have possibly come within the range of a periodical visit from ships laden with merchandise, the roadstead affording as good an anchorage as, or even better than, that possessed formerly by Madras. The coins of Rome, China, and other distant lands, found till recently in the débris, give us good reason to believe that when the Ephesians were worshipping in the ancient temple erected to the great Goddess Diana, the people of Tarsis and of Phœnicia and of the isles thereof resorted to the Coromandel Coast for barter. Moreover, Chinese and other coins often washed ashore in storms evidence the supposition that this was one of the centres of Eastern trade, a port frequented by foreign ships, of which some must have been wrecked and sunk in the vicinity. The discovery of large deposits of ancient bricks form sufficient ground for the belief that here there was an ancient city built some two centuries before the Christian Era, having commercial relations with foreign countries. Buddhist remains point to the attraction this same city must have had even for the peoples of this land. But who is able to tie the harness and weave with tinsel the beautiful-bordered romance of the "Wave-covered Metropolis of Bali"? The temple so close to the sea that the waves foam and dash against its doorway, and the presence of large quantities of stone which partially appeared buried in the water, indicate that in the days when the Mahabarata was written, buildings existed which have become destroyed and overwhelmed by the ocean's encroachment. But whether caused by tides or by earthquake, whether the action was gradual or sudden, whether Chandra and Surya conspired together to overthrow the city, matters not to the visitor. He reads in that solitary temple standing on the shore the last page of the story anterior to the events that followed and are interpreted by the monumental records situated inland. Even here, though the outward form of the Pagodas is complete, the ultimate design has not been accomplished, but seems to have been defeated by some convulsion in nature or in human society.

The poetical talent of Southey has immortalised the ancient city in the following lines:

THE CITY OF BALI

I.

Their talk was of the city of the days
Of old Earth's wonder once, and of the fame
Of Bali, its great founder . . . he whose name
In ancient story and in poet's praise

Liveth and flourisheth for endless glory
Because his might
Put down the wrong and aye upheld the right
Till for ambition, as old sages tell,
At length the Universal Monarch fell:
For he, too, having made the world his own,
Then in his pride had driven
The Devotas from Heaven,
And seized triumphantly the Swerga Throne.
The incarnate came before the Mighty One,
In dwarfish stature and in mien obscure;
The sacred cord he bore,
And asked, for Brama's sake, a little boon:
Three steps of Bali's ample reign, no more.
Poor was the boon required, and poor was he
Who begg'd—a little wretch it seemed to be;
But Bali ne'er refused a suppliant's prayer.
He on the Dwarf cast down
A glance of pity in contemptuous mood,
And bade him take the boon,
And measure where he would.

2.

Lo, Son of Giant birth,
I take my grant! the Incarnate Power replies.
With this first step he measured o'er the Earth,
The second spann'd the skies.
Three paces thou hast granted,
Twice have I set my footstep, Veshnoo cries,
Where shall the third be planted?

3.

Then Bali knew the God, and at his feet,
In homage due, he laid his humbled head.

Mighty art thou, O Lord of Earth and Heaven,
Mighty art thou ! he said.
Be merciful, and let me be forgiven,
He ask'd for mercy of the Merciful,
And mercy for his virtue's sake was shown.
For though he was cast down to Padalon,
Yet there, by Yamen's throne,
Doth Bali sit in majesty and might,
To judge the dead and sentence them aright.
And forasmuch as he was still the friend
Of righteousness, it is permitted him,
Yearly, from those drear regions to ascend
And walk the Earth, that he may hear his name
Still hymn'd and honoured by the grateful voice
Of humankind, and in his fame rejoice.

4.

Such was the talk they held upon their way
Of him to whose old City they were bound ;
And now, upon their journey, many a day
Had risen and closed, and many a week gone round,
And many a realm and region had they pass'd
When now the Ancient Towers appear'd at last.

5.

Their golden summits in the noonday light
Shone o'er the dark green deep that roll'd between,
For domes, and pinnacles, and spires were seen
Peering above the sea—a mournful sight !
Well might the sad beholder ween from thence
What works of wonder the devouring wave
Had swallow'd there, when monuments so brave
Bore record of their old magnificence.

And on the sandy shore, beside the verge
  Of ocean, here and there, a rock-hewn fane
Resisted in its strength the surf and surge
  That on their deep foundations beat in vain.
In solitude the Ancient Temples stood,
  Once resonant with instrument and song
And solemn dance of festive multitude ;
  Now as the weary ages pass along,
Hearing no voice save the ocean flood,
Which roars for ever on the restless shores ;
  Or visiting their solitary caves,
The lonely sound of winds, that moan around
  Accordant to the melancholy waves.

BRAHMINICAL ACCOUNT OF THE ORIGIN OF THE PLACE

The account which the Brahmans give of its origin and downfall may seem worthy of attention. "Hiranyakasipu, a gigantic prince, refused to do homage to Vishnu. He had a son named Prahlada, who at an early age openly disapproved this part of his father's conduct, being under the tuition of Sukracharya. His father persecuted him on this account, and banished him. At length Hiranyakasipu was softened and recalled his son to his Court, where as he sat in full assembly he began again to argue with him against the supremacy of Vishnu, boasted that he himself was lord of all the Visible World, and asked what Vishnu could pretend to more. Prahlada replied that Vishnu had no fixed abode but was present everywhere. 'Is he,' said his father, 'in that pillar?' 'Yes,' returned Prahlada. 'Then let him come forth,' said Hiranyakasipu; and rising from his seat struck the pillar with his foot, upon which Vishnu, in the Narasimha Avatara—that is to say, with a body like a man, but a head like a lion—came out of the pillar, and tore Hiranyakasipu in pieces. Vishnu then fixed Prahlada on his father's throne. He left a son, inherited his power and his virtues, and was the father of Bali, the founder of the once magnificent city of Mahabalipura."

Such is the Brahman account of the origin of this place. The sequel of its history, according to them, is as follows:

"The son of Bali was Banasura, who is represented as a giant with a thousand hands. Aniruddha, the grandson of Krishna, came to his Court in disguise and seduced his daughter, which produced a war, in the course of which Aniruddha was taken prisoner, and brought to Mahabalipura, upon which Krishna came in person from his capital Dwaraka, and laid siege to the place. Siva guarded the gates, and fought for Banasura, who worshipped him with his thousand hands; but Krishna found means to overthrow Siva, and, having taken the city, cut off all Banasura's hands, except two, with which he obliged him to do homage. He continued in subjection to Krishna till his death; after which a long period ensued, in which no mention is anywhere made of this place, till a prince arose, whose name was Malecheren, who restored the kingdom to great splendour. Malecheren (say they), in an excursion which he made one day alone and in disguise, came to a garden in the environs of the city, where was a fountain so inviting that two celestial nymphs had come down to bathe there. The Raja became enamoured of one of them, who condescended to allow of his attachment to her ; and she and her sister-nymph used thenceforward to have frequent interviews with him in that garden. On one of those occasions they brought with them a male inhabitant of the heavenly regions, to whom they introduced the Raja ; and between him and Malecheren a strict friendship ensued, in consequence of which he agreed, at the Raja's earnest request, to carry him in disguise to see the Court of the divine Indra, a favour never before granted to any mortal. The Raja returned from thence with new ideas of splendour and magnificence, which he immediately adopted in regulating his Court and his retinue, and in beautifying his seat of government. By this means Mahabalipura became soon celebrated beyond all the cities of the earth ; and an account of its magnificence having been brought to the Gods assembled at the Court of Indra, their jealousy was so much excited at it, that they sent orders to the God of the sea to let loose his billows and overflow a place which impiously pretended to vie in splendour with their celestial mansions. This command he obeyed, and the city was at once overflowed by that furious element, nor has it ever since been able to rear its head."

Such is the mode in which the Brahmans choose to account for the signal overthrow of the place.

THE SEVEN PAGODAS

Mamallapuram or the Seven Pagodas is about thirty-five miles south of Madras, and lies between the coast and the Buckingham Canal. A most enjoyable trip is to do it by boat, leaving Madras about nightfall, and reaching the place early in the morning. An alternative route is to travel by the South Indian Railway as far as Chingleput, and thence to proceed by Jutka to the Seven Pagodas, a distance of eighteen miles which can be done in two and a half hours. One limited to time can do it by motor-car, the distance being thirty-five miles from Madras to Chingleput, and eighteen from Chingleput to Mahabalipuram. There is a fairly good metalled road right up to the canal, and a ferry-boat is always available to take one across. On the south there is a rest-house with accommodation for about six persons, where food is procurable if intimation is sent previously.

NAME OF THE PLACE AND ITS ORIGIN

The place is known to Europeans by the name of the Seven Pagodas, because it is believed that at one time there stood some such number of Pagodas on the shore whose tops, covered with copper, reflected the sun's rays and served as a landmark for mariners. At present there is only one shore temple. The Hindu distinguishes the place by three names according to the origin he accepts:

1. *Mahamalaipur.*—The city of the great mountain, Maha referring to greatness of sanctity or renown.

2. *Mamallapuram*, or Mallapuri (as in the Sthala purana or local legend), the name being

derived from its founder, an offset of the Malla Chieftains in the north who had been subdued and driven out of their possessions by the Chalukyan dynasty. Mahamalla occurs as a surname of the Pallava King Narasimha Varman I. who founded the city.

3. *Mavalipuram* with its equivalent in sanscrit, Mahabalipuram, or the city of the Great Bali, the name of a hero famous in Hindu romance. Southey, in his "Curse of Kehama," notices it by this last name. Mamallapuram, however, is the most authoritative form of the name. (*Vide* Appendix.)

TIME OF EXECUTION

The temples were executed by the conquered Chalukyas from the north under the auspices of the Pallava Kings, who had their capital at Conjeeveram in the beginning of the fourth century, and gradually extended their sway to the middle of the eighth century. Many of them were executed between A.D. 600-625, and bear a striking resemblance to some of the sculptures at Ellora executed under the Chalukyas of that

THE RATHAS

period. The Chalukyas only temporarily resided here, and were driven out of the country after a struggle permanently and for ever. They must have been numerous and powerful, for in the short interval that elapsed between their inception and abandonment they created works which, considering the hardness of the granite rocks in which they were executed, may fairly be termed gigantic. Yet there is no trace of any city in the neighbourhood which they could have inhabited.

The antiquities are divided into three groups :

1. The five so-called Rathas to the south of the village belonging to the latest Buddhist period. (The sanscrit word *Ratha* means a car, these temples being supposed to resemble cars on which idols are dragged in procession, but the word is a misnomer.)

2. Cave temples, monolithic figures, carvings and sculptures, west of the village (sixth and seventh century).

3. Modern temples of Vishnu and Siva, the latter being washed by the sea.

THE FIVE RATHAS

These Rathas were probably intended to serve the purpose of temples, but bear marks of having been left in an unfinished state. They bear the names of the five Pandava brothers and their common lawful wife—Draupadi.

The Square Rathas are copies of Buddhist Viharas, or monasteries, and are the originals from which all the Vimanas (the structure standing over the shrine) of Southern India were copied. The oblong Rathas were Chaityas, or assembly halls or porticoes with the Buddhists, and became the type for the modern Gopurams or gateways which are frequently more important parts of Dravidian temples than the Vimanas themselves.

THE NAKULA AND SAHADEVA RATHA—(1)

The first of these Rathas with the apsidal termination called Sahadeva and Nakula's Ratha (the youngest two of the five Pandava brothers)

NAKULA AND SAHADEVA'S RATHAS

DRAUPADI RATHA

stands a little detached ; it is in shape similar to a horseshoe, and is an example of a Buddhist Chaitya.

The other four temples stand in a line and look as if they had been carved out of a single rock. Between the detached temple and these four there is an elephant and a lion carved out of single blocks of stone, and east of it is a Nandi bull (the vehicle of Siva).

DRAUPADI RATHA—(2)

The most northern of the four is known as the Draupadi Ratha. It represents a Pansala, or cell, cut out of solid rock for the abode of one of the chief priests. The priests were not allowed to lie down, but were obliged to pass the night in a sitting posture. At the entrance are two female doorkeepers with Buddhist head-dress and emblems. It has no throne or image internally, but there is the figure of Lakshmi.

ARJUNA'S RATHA—(3)

This is a copy of terraced Buddhist Vihara, and is of a pyramidal shape. Its dimensions are 11 × 16 × 20 feet, and is three-storied. It is a small copy of the last Ratha to the southward.

BHIMA'S RATHA—(4)

It is an oblong building with a curvilinear-shaped roof with a straight edge, 42 × 25 × 25 feet high. There is a veranda facing the west, supported by four pillars, ornamented at the base with the horned lion, the "Pallava" type of pillar. It is cracked through the centre, and the theory is that it is due to the unskilfulness of the northern workmen who fashioned it, in a first attempt, after a structural building of the same class with pillars to support an ordinary wooden roof. In this case, the roof being of solid granite, the supports were insufficient, and the crack was a hint for the builders to stop work.

The "wagon roof" form of this Ratha is strikingly like the shape of the huts used by the

Kurumbars of the Nilgiris to the present day. This seems to point to the fact that the Kurumbars are the living representatives of the Pallavas, and that they were associated as labourers with the Chalukyas, the master-sculptors.

DHARMA RAJA'S RATHA—(5)

This is the most interesting of the monolithic temples. It is 27 × 25 × 34 feet high, and is four-storied, with a central portico facing the west, having two pillars with the horned lion at the base, and at each corner there is a male guardian or deity. The fourth story is dome-shaped with eight sides, and on the second, third, and fourth stories are seated figures of men in the usual attitude of Buddha concealed behind ranges of simulated cells. There are eighteen in the lowest story, fourteen round the second, and ten round the third. On this shrine are two parapets for the performance of Prodakshina, which is a reverential mode of salutation by circumambulating a person or object with the right side turned towards them. We have in this Ratha most of the Hindu Pantheon—Brahma, Vishnu and Siva—in forms more subdued than is to be found elsewhere in India. There are inscriptions over the majority of them, and they are merely epithets applicable to the figures over which they are placed. They give no information as to date or origin.

THE MAHISHAMARDINI MANTAPAM—(6)

Retracing one's steps from the Rathas, the first object of interest is an excavated temple situated below the summit of the most southern eminence of the ridge where the lighthouse is built. It is known as the Yamapuri ("the city of Yama," the God of death) or Mahishamardini Mantapam, Parvati or Durga being the slayer of Mahisha. The excavation contains three niches, of which the centre one is the principal, with a portal before it, and containing a group of figures representing Mahadeva, Parvati, and their infant son Subramaniya. Between Mahadeva and Parvati is Vishnu in his four-armed form, holding the Sanka (couch), the Chakra (disc), and the Gada (mace). On the right side of Mahadeva is

DHARMA RAJA'S RATHA

PANEL OF ARTHANARISWARA IN DHARMA RAJA'S RATHA

FIGURE HALF MALE AND HALF FEMALE, SIVA AND PARVATI COMBINED

PANEL OF VISHNU IN MAHISHAMARDANI CAVE

Brahma with four faces. The bull Nandi is in front of the principal figure, and on its back rests one foot of Mahadeva and one of Parvati. The excavation is chiefly remarkable for the sculptures executed on its side walls. One represents Vishnu's state of existence, and the other the celebrated conflict between Durga and Mahishasura. On the left panel Vishnu appears as Narayana or Ranganayaka in the act of willing creation. Under this character Vishnu is represented lying in a Yogi trance on the lotus as well as on the thousand-headed serpent Sesha, whose coils form a pillow, while five of its heads form a canopy. Above the God are two small figures, celestial musicians, male and female, and below him in front, in a kneeling position, are three figures, two of whom are cowherds (husband and wife) who had come to complain to Vishnu. Before they do so, they inquire of the third figure — the sorcerer — about the propitious opportunity for a visit. While making the inquiry, one of the attendants of Mahishasura bears a club to punish them for daring to appeal to Vishnu, and the other figure interposes and drives away from his master's presence the presumptuous servant of the wicked Mahishasura.

The Durga and Mahishasura relief on the right wall is one of the most artistic and spirited reliefs to be seen, and depicts the victory of active good over evil. The Goddess Durga, mounted on a lion, overpowers evil personified in the buffalo-headed demon Mahishasura, who grasps a short thick club. The figure of Durga is five feet high and eight-handed. Two of her arms have greater relief than the others, a circumstance which imparts to the figure a much greater appearance to truth and nature than would otherwise be the case. The principal arm is stretched at full length and the hand grasps a bow, the right arm is drawn back as if in the act of discharging an arrow, but we see neither the arrow nor the string of the bow. Her six remaining hands hold respectively on the left, a bell, a Sanka, and something else not easily distinguishable, and on the right the fatal cord, the Chakra (disc) and a sword. Full of life and movement, the Goddess forms a dignified figure around her attendant warriors. There are also two domestics, one with a switch of hair such as horsekeepers use and the other with an umbrella. Durga's attendants are all dwarfish, corpulent figures, those of Mahishasura seem of more natural proportion.

PANEL OF MAHISHAMARDANI

ROCK CUT TEMPLE (page 37).

Of three figures between the principal personages two are in conflict and the third is falling headlong.

In reference to this subject, Sir William Jones writes the following lines :

> "O Durga, thou hast deign'd to shield
> Man's feeble virtue with celestial might,
> Gliding from your jasper field,
> And, on a lion borne, hast brav'd the fight ;
> For when the demon Vice thy realms defied,
> And arm'd with death each arched horn,
> Thy golden lance, O Goddess mountain born,
> Touch but the pest, he roar'd and died."

OLAKKANNESVARASWAMI TEMPLE—(11)

Above this Mantapam dedicated to Durga is the temple of Olakkannesvaraswami. When this city flourished, small fanam (three-fourths of an anna) used to be collected from each shop making a quarter measureful (Olakku) of fanams for the God in this temple. The God has rolled away somewhere, and they say that if the jungle below is cut down the Linga will be found. On account of its position, this structure was used as a lighthouse before the present one was built.

KRISHNA'S MANTAPAM—(15)

Coming down by the Zamindar's bungalow and opposite to a street in the village is the Krishna Mantapam, or choultry, of later date than any of the other excavations. The sculptures on the back wall represent the exploit of Krishna supporting the mountain Govardhana (about fourteen miles from Muttra) in order to shelter Nanda and his followers, the cowherds, from a storm created by Indra as a test of Krishna's divinity. The cowherd Nanda is the reputed foster-father of Krishna.

The God appears to sustain the mountain with the palm of his left hand, the only representation of the supported mountain consisting of a rough line running above the whole of the figures. This line has been formed by cutting away as much of the rock as would answer the purpose of giving the necessary degree of relief for typifying the rugged bottom of the mountain torn up from its foundations and sustained aloft in the air. On the left of the God are three female figures, one of these having a pot of curds on her head. On Krishna's right is Balarama, his half-brother. His

KRISHNA MANTAPAM

left hand is on a cowherd, and he is standing with one foot advanced. To the right of Balarama is a cowherd milking a cow in the act of licking its calf. Above is a small figure of Krishna playing on his flute to collect the cows. In this form he is called Balakrishnan, and is reputed to have amused himself by piping to the swains and damsels of Govardhana. In front of the cow is a woman carrying a mortar and holding in her hand a net containing pots of curds. On the right stands Nandi, a milk-white bull, the name of Siva's vehicle. It is a symbol of the deity's generative powers and of Dharma, righteousness. The bull is here seen with head slightly turned and forefoot extended as if suddenly startled. It is one of the finest and most natural bulls ever seen sculptured. Several interesting particulars regarding the ancient Hindus may be gathered from this pastoral scene. The dress of the females resembles that now worn by the Nairs and Tiyans on the west coast, who are uncovered above the waist. The men wore turbans, and the women very large ear-rings, with bangles on their hands and feet. The peculiar practice of carrying the infant on the hip was then in use, and even the vertical arrangement and method of tying together the three earthen vessels here represented is recognised as being universally adopted by the modern Gopalas (cowherds).

The execution of this work is coarse and the design rude, the proportions are bad and the countenances are destitute of expression. It may be that the general quietude and repose of the figures are intended to imply their security from the terrible danger so recently and still, but for the God's interposition, impending over them.

At the north end of this sculpture, raised five or six feet from the floor, is a well-executed figure of a Brahmany bull (Nandi) in full relief, and at the south end are several figures of beasts apparently intended for lions ; one of them, however, resembles the sphinx with a human face and the body of a quadruped.

ARJUNA'S PENANCE—(17)

A few yards north on the east face of the ridge will be found sculptured in bas-relief on the faces of two large rocks the story of the intense penance of Arjuna. The two rocks measure 96 feet by 43 feet, and are divided by a fissure, and the cleft is

skilfully used to show a Naga or Snake God, and a Nagini and other snake deities as coming up from the depths of ocean drawn by the ascetic's magnetic power to pay him homage. Mr. Fergusson remarks that it may well be that the magnificent bas-relief commemorates the attempt to engraft the tolerant religion of the Buddhists on the faith of a nation of worshippers of the great serpent God. No amount of preaching nor any height of eloquence could possibly reach the sublime effect of this sermon in stone teaching peace and goodwill. In this group of sculptures, the principal figure Arjuna is seen on the left of the fissure in the posture of penance. He stands on the great toe of the left foot. His chest and ribs are prominent, and his arms and right leg appear withered. The figure of a four-armed deity standing by him holding the Pasupathasthra (a fabulous weapon), Damaruka (small drum), and Trisula (trident), and attended by dwarfs, seems to be that of Siva, and between him and Arjuna stands Visvakarma (the son of Brahma and architect of the Gods) with an adze on his right shoulder. Above are Surya, Chandra, etc., and immediately below is a small temple of Vishnu with devotees. To the right is Drona-Charya, the preceptor of the Kauravas and Pandavas, seated in the lotus posture doing penance with thighs crossed, one hand resting on the left thigh, the other held up with the thumb upon the heart, the eyes being directed to the tip of the nose.

The upper part of both rocks is covered with a great crowd of celestials, Gods and Sages, the Ghandarvas (heavenly musicians with bird-like legs), and various four-footed denizens of the Hindu Olympus, who are hastening to watch the wonderful penance.

The right-hand rock is distinguished by a magnificent group of elephants—Indra's noble beasts—realistically treated. The foremost tusker (measuring 17 feet by 14 feet) gives shelter to a delightful group of baby elephants, while the female elephant impatiently waits her turn behind him in the procession.

Just below the tusks of the big elephant is the figure of a cat on its hind-legs, with its fore-paws raised above its head in seeming imitation of Arjuna performing penance—after eating part of Krishna's butter-ball—in order that the sea may dry up so that she may be able to devour all the fish. Near the cat are rats enjoying apparently their temporary immunity from persecution.

DETAILS FROM ARJUNA'S PENANCE (page 42).

THE STORY OF ARJUNA'S PENANCE

The story of Arjuna's penance is from the Mahabarata, and it is a typical one for illustrating the Hindu belief in the virtue of ascetic practices for gaining extraordinary psychic powers. The story is as follows : The five sons of Pandu Rajah lost their dominions with their cousin Duriyodhana, who played unfairly. The consequence was that they and their followers were banished for twelve years to wander in jungles. At the end of this period, when the struggle of the Pandavas and Kauravas was impending, Arjuna, on the advice of his brother Yudhisthira, set out to the north of the Himalaya Mountains to obtain the Pasupathasthra, or celestial weapons, guarded by Indra. He was armed with Krishna's famous bow. Moved by Arjuna's constancy, Indra consented to yield to him the celestial arms, when Siva, the highest of all the Gods, should deign to reveal himself to him. Arjuna reached an auspicious spot on the banks of a foaming river. The first month he subsisted by eating fruits at intervals of three nights, next he increased the intervals to six nights, and then to fourteen days. By the fourth month he began to exist on air alone. The tremendous energy produced by his mental concentration began to disturb the cosmic order, and all the great sages went in agitation to complain to Siva, who meets him in combat as rival hunters over a boar struck down, and admiring him for his valour, gave him the weapon with which he should overcome his enemies.

A short distance on the right is a group of monkeys, originally consisting of a male, a female, and a young one. The male monkey with a laudable love of cleanliness is studying the head of its partner with the most friendly attention.

PANCHAPANDAVAS' MANTAPAM—(16)

Adjoining Arjuna's penance to the south are the beginnings of an excavation known as the Mantapam of the five Pandavas. It has a front of 50 feet and a depth of about 40 feet, with deep recesses on either side in which stone has been left rough cut for three pillars. The front is supported by two rows of octagonal columns whose bases are formed of figures of a grotesque horned animal. The

GANESA TEMPLE

capitals of these columns are not unlike those of some of the pillars at Ellora and of the cave-temples of Elephanta in Bombay.

GANESA TEMPLE—(19)

North-west of Arjuna's penance is Ganesa's Ratha cut out of a single stone in which Siva was placed, and when that Linga was carried off, the people took an image of Ganesa and put it in. The temple measures 20 × 11½ × 28 feet high, and has three stories. The top is elliptical, and bears a resemblance to the Gothic style. The pillars of the base which support a veranda on the western side are of very slender and wooden form. It gives a fair idea of the form their oblong temples took.

RAMANUJA MANTAPAM—(19a)

South of Ganesa's temple and almost hidden from view is an excavation in the side of the hill. In the middle are two pillars, but there are no figures in it. At the bases of the pillars are four lions' heads. On the south side of it are thirteen steps cut out of the rocky hill. There is a short inscription on the floor.

EXCAVATION WITH VARAHA AND VAMANA INCARNATIONS—(20)

Near to this on the south, and facing west, is a Mantapam hollowed out of solid rock, known as the Varahaswami temple. In the sanctuary are no figures, but there are two doorkeepers.

VARAHA AVATARA—(3rd Incarnation)

On the wall to the left is the Varaha, or Boar incarnation of Vishnu, which is executed with considerable spirit. His right foot rests on the head of the thousand-headed serpent with its hands raised in prayer, its lower part being immersed in what may be supposed a representation of the waves of the sea. Lakshmi is seated on his right thigh facing him. His right hand is on her hinder part, his left hand holds her right leg, while the two other hands hold the

VARAHA AVATARA

VARAHASWAMI TEMPLE

conch and the disc. The God and the Goddess are regarding each other, and he with his boar mouth is in playful dalliance kissing her. Behind him is a four-armed male warrior. Facing this figure is that of a woman. Above these two is a votary with joined hands, and three votaries praising Varahaswami.

It may be asked, Why did Vishnu assume the boar form? The story runs that a Daitya or evil spirit named Hiranyaksha ("Golden Eye") gained from Brahma, by his scrupulous piety, a promise that he should have given to him anything he asked. He desired universal dominion and exemption from being hurt by the bite or power of any living creature. He enumerated all animals but forgot the boar. His ambitious desires were no sooner obtained than he became exceedingly presumptuous, and, forgetting the great power of the Gods, ran away with the whole earth, and plunged it and himself into the depths of the sea, when Vishnu intervened and raised the earth above the flood. The sculptures illustrative of the story appear to refer to a period subsequent to the battle, for the figures supply the imagination with the idea that the boar-headed deity is now solacing himself after the toils and dangers of his thousand years' conflict.

To the left of the east wall is Lakshmi on her lotus throne, rising from the sea of milk. Mr. Havell, who looks at things with a spiritual vision, interprets this panel thus: Lakshmi represents fertility and earthly prosperity arising from the cosmic ocean when churned by the Gods. The Goddess rises from the waves on a full-blown lotus flower, attended by Ganga and other river deities. Indra's elephants, the mighty monsoon clouds, bring their precious water in golden vessels and pour them over her, the Queen of the Universe. Lakshmi, when rising from the waves, gazes with undisguised rapture and wonderment upon the apparition of Vishnu. Full of adoration for her divine spouse, she prepares to throw herself upon his breast.

To the right of this on the east wall is a four-armed Durga holding an umbrella. On one side there are three attendants carrying swords and a deer, and on the other three armed attendants and a lion. There is also one doorkeeper.

PANEL OF LAKSHMI WITH ELEPHANTS IN VARAHA CAVE

VAMANA AVATARA

VAMANA AVATARA—(5th Incarnation)

On the south wall is the eight-armed Trivikrama (three-stepper), as Vishnu is known, holding the conch, the disc, and the mace. It is known as the Vamana, or Dwarf incarnation of Vishnu. This incarnation was undertaken to recover heaven for the Gods. Bali, a demon, was King over the three worlds—heaven, earth, and sky. He was so elated by his prosperity that he omitted to perform the more essential sacrifices to the Gods. Vishnu, to check so bad an example, became incarnate, and assumed the form of a Brahman Dwarf. He appeared before the King, who said, "Welcome to thee, O Brahman! What can we do for thee?" The Dwarf concludes a speech with the semblance of moderation as follows: "I ask from thee a small portion of ground, three paces measured step by step. I desire no more from thee. A wise man incurs no sin when he asks only as much as he needs." This the King granted, and began to ratify his promise by pouring water into the petitioner's hand. As he was doing this immediately the pigmy became a Giant, and with one step strode over heaven, and with the second over the earth, and there was nowhere for him to take a third, and as Vishnu reproached Bali to find a place for the third, Bali offered his head, and with the third he pushed him into the lower world, said to be the abode of the serpent. He then gave the empire of the world to Indra, and thus fulfilled his purpose. Some believe that the water used in this transaction for the purpose of ratification fell from Vishnu's hand on the head of Siva, and, flowing thence, formed the origin of the Ganges.

It is said that Sukra, regent of the planet Venus and Guru of the Asuras, acting as minister of Bali, informed the King of the deceit that was being practised upon him. There is a figure with a dog-like head speaking to another, who seems to rest his chin on his right hand in deep reflection. These two figures occupy the upper part of the sculpture on the left of Vishnu. Below them are two figures in human shape represented as falling. Perhaps the former may represent Sukra and Bali at the moment when the prince was first made acquainted by his counsellor with the true character of the Dwarf, but was too proud to withdraw his loyal pledge; and the latter the same after he had fallen from his high estate.

Panel of Durga with Umbrella in Varaha Cave (page 48).

Some people interpret the three steps of Vishnu to represent the different positions of the sun (Vishnu) : at his rising, his culmination, and his setting. Frequently in the Rig Veda the term "wide-stepping" is applied to him. Mr. Havell, who looks at it from this point of view, explains the sculpture and criticises it thus: Vishnu, the all-pervading soul of the Universe, is represented upholding the heaven with one arm and filling space with all the attributes of his glory. Seated at his feet are four genii, the guardians of his paradise-symbolising the four quarters of the earth. Vishnu stands for the sun in its midday splendour as representing the principle of all life. On the right and left are smaller figures of Brahma and Siva on their heavenly lotus thrones as symbols of the sun's rising and setting. The "strides of Vishnu," or the apparent movement of the sun across the heavens, are suggested by the upraised leg and outstretched figure of one hand, which Siva is touching.

"Notice," says he, "the splendid vigour and imaginative power of the artist. The bold generalisation is free from over-elaboration. The stately uprightness of the body of the deity is echoed by the mighty lines of the bow and sword and by the slightly varied attitude of the four genii in a massive relief which contrasts with telling effect against the vigorous movement of the outstretched arms. The ascending and descending movement of the smaller figures on the left balances the whole composition in lower planes of relief, which finely symbolise the gradual dawn and close of day at the Sun's rising and setting. The spiritual signification of the attributes as represented by symbols are thus interpreted. The gem in his necklace is the pure soul of the world.

"The bow and the spiral conch represent the principle of consciousness.

"The shafts from the bow represent the faculties of action and perception.

"The bright sword in the right arm is holy wisdom.

"The mace is the power of intellect, and the discus the wonder-working, effulgent power.

"The curl on the breast is the principle of things, and his necklace of five gems—pearl, ruby, emerald, sapphire, and diamond—are the five elemental rudiments."

STHALASAYANA SWAMI TEMPLE—(22)

In front of Krishna's Mantapam, from which it is divided by a road, is the modern temple of the village dedicated to Vishnu and known as the Sthalasayana Swami temple, so called because in it the God is represented in a lying posture with his feet to the north. This is the principal sanctuary, and to the north of it, in the temple area, is a sanctuary dedicated to the Goddess Sudikoduthal, so called because she first wore in her hair the flowers she intended to offer to the God. Legends have been invented to attract pilgrims to these modern Vishnu temples, in which the sin-destroying virtues of Mallapuri have been extolled.

DOLOTSAVA MANTAPAM—(23)

In front of the modern temple is the Dolotsava Mantapam ("porch of the swinging festival"), where the image of God used annually to be brought out and swung before the people. It is of granite, and is supported on four columns which rise from a platform elevated by three steps. The Mantapam is remarkable for the lightness and elegance of its construction.

THE SHORE TEMPLE—(25)

This is an old Dravidian temple (one of the remains of the Seven Pagodas believed to be submerged in the sea by an earthquake) built about the ninth century, and has attracted most attention from travellers because of its lonely and unique position on the seashore, where it is within range of the spray from the surf. It is surrounded on three sides by a granite screen on which are figures of forty-six stone bulls closely set. It stops short in the west side, where stands a miniature of the temple opening towards the west and bearing every appearance of having originally been its principal entrance, but it seems to have been afterwards converted into a separate shrine, and the passage of communication between the two has been blocked up at each end. The temple is in the purest Dravidian style, the Vimana or tower over the shrine forming the central and principal mass, while the Gopuram, or the original gateway (now the smaller shrine), is comparatively insignificant. The later Dravidian style displays the Gopuram as the chief architectural feature of a temple, thus revealing the workings of the human mind to be the same the whole world over, and which

A STHAMBA OR LAMP-POST IN THE SEA OPPOSITE DOORWAY OF SHORE TEMPLE (page 55).

led the master-builders of the west to emphasise the porches of the Cathedral rather than the east end.

The height of the larger Vimana is about 60 feet, and, like the smaller one, it is surmounted by the umbrella-shaped summit called Kalasa, made of black basaltic rock which, unlike the granite below, bears no signs of destruction by the sea air. Mr. Fergusson declares it to be with the single exception of the Pagoda at Tanjore, the finest and most important Vimana in the south of India. A doorway cut in the screen overlooks the sea, and below is a steep and rugged rock washed by the breakers. This rock has the appearance of having been partly cut into rude steps, and partly perforated as if to receive some platform or superstructure that has since disappeared. One solitary column still raises its head above the waves and is commonly considered to have been a Sthamba or lamp-post, which is found fronting all Hindu temples. The ground inland had obviously been built over to a considerable extent. The foundations of ancient walls have been dug out, and most of the houses in the village are built of these old bricks.

Within this temple will be found a large broken black granite Lingam sixteen-sided, and a group of sculptures in a recess on the central wall representing Mahadeva (Siva), Parvati, and their son Subrahmaniya. On the two sides are Brahma and Vishnu. The smaller temple contains a similar group of figures, the Tirumurti. In a sort of veranda or dark cell behind, formed by the space within the second wall (the seven-walled Siva temple showing only traces of two walls), lies Sri Maha Vishnu with his head to the south, and with the ordinary Sesha, Naga (King of the serpent race, a large thousand-headed snake, at once the couch and canopy of Vishnu and the upholder of the world), which rests on one of his heads below and above him.

The unusual presence of the two deities under one roof can only be explained by presuming that the temple was erected before the intolerance of sects had produced irreconcilable antagonism between the Sivite and Vaishnavite faiths.

Visitors are advised to see this temple not only by day but also by night, about the time of the full moon, when solitude reigns and the moon with its sparkling radiance lights up the waters of the sea, and the sound of the roaring waves is heard as they cast their foam within a few fathoms off the sacred mound. The deity of the waters seems to revel then in delight, while the mild effulgence of

Panel of Siva in the Tirumurthi Cave (page 56).

Panel of Tirumurthi in the Shrine Niche of Shore Temple–West (page 56).

THE SHORE TEMPLE (page 56).

KRISHNA'S BUTTER BALL (page 57).

he silvery moon filtering through the open door of the edifice bewitches the human senses into ingering ecstasy. The sea bubbles with pleasure at the sight of his offspring Chandra, who, being born at the churning of the ocean, supplies the note of triumph that lifts the scene above the commonplace at the touch of the enchantress's wand.

KRISHNA'S BUTTER-BALL—(31)

In the middle of the hill on the face of a rock is a large round butter-ball made by Draupadi, and known as Krishna's Butter-Ball, for the pat of butter was petrified by the God of milkmaids—Krishnan. Half of this is said to have been eaten by a cat, which gives the ball a chipped appearance. The cat is seen, with its fore-paws upraised, tied to the hill on which Arjuna is performing penance. Near this point a spectator looking southwards in the lengthening shadows of the evening may see, formed by the ridges on which the caves are cut, the recumbent figure of a man with his hands in the attitude of prayer. This is called the Giant Raja Bali, and is the work of the Jains.

DHARMARAJA'S LION THRONE—(32)

Farther south on the top of the hill is the fine gateway of a Vishnu temple, known as the Rayala Gopuram, Rayala being the title of the princes of Vijayanagara. It measures 66 feet in length, and 42 in breadth. In the middle of this is a gateway running east and west, and at the corners are five stone pillars delicately carved with floral ornaments. This Gopuram and the modern temple of Vishnu form nearly a straight line with the shore temple. Nearly opposite to this gateway is Dharmaraja's Lion Throne, where some prince of that name was wont to dispense justice to his people, and the turmeric bath of Draupadi, the lawful wife of the Pandavas. Tradition has it that near this place a palace was recently built, and there are signs of bricks, etc., about the place.

DHARMA RAJA'S LION THRONE

APPENDIX

I.—NAME OF THE PLACE AND ITS ORIGIN

As noted in the "Imperial Gazetteer of India" (Article "Seven Pagodas," vol. xxii., p. 182), the vernacular name is variously spelt as Mahabālipur, Mahāvellipur, Mavallipur, Mamalaipur, Mamallapur, and Malaipur.

Mr. Crole, in his "Chingleput Manual," mentions that the name in Tamil is (1) Mahabalipuram, (2) Mavallipuram, (3) Mamalaipuram, or more properly Mammallapuram, and in the Sthalapurana Mallapuri, and that the two latter give the true name of which the others are corruptions or misnomers applied through ignorance. He refers to an inscription relating to a King Amara (?), who overcame Pallava Mardu, and was entitled to the name "Raja Malla," having, as the inscription states, "secured his acquisition by his large and strong arms, and conquered the chief (Palaka) of the Mahamalla race." Mr. Crole considers that this inscription must be of a date about A.D. 620, and that it gives a clear indication of the origin of the title Malla. "There is no doubt that this was the name of a family of a powerful highland chieftain, who had been subdued by the Chalukyans. But the connection in which the word occurs in the above inscription favours the supposition that it was also the name of the Pallava clan occupying this part of the Carnatic."

What appears to be the latest and most authoritative contribution to the question of the origin of the name occurs in a learned article on the Pallavas, contributed by the late Rai Bahadur V. Venkayya to the annual report of the Archæological Survey of India for 1906-07 (pp. 217-243). I reproduce below Mr. Venkayya's remarks (p. 233):

"About the *Rathas* at the Seven Pagodas, Mr. Fergusson says: 'On the whole it seems more probable that their date is somewhat earlier than 700, but their execution may have been spread over half a century or even more, so that absolute precision is impossible in the present state of the evidence. Still, until some fixed date or some new information is afforded, 650 to 700 may, probably, be safely relied upon as very nearly that at which the granite rocks at Mahavallipur were carved into the wondrous forms which still excite our admiration there. This, then, is the approximate date of the construction of the *Rathas* erivable from a study of the sculptures and the architecture. Let us see if epigraphical research helps us towards a closer approximation. The popular name of the Seven Pagodas is Mavala-auram, which is believed to connect the town with the demon Mahabali, overpowered by the God Vishnu in his *Vamana Avatara* or Dwarf ncarnation. Mr. Rice is of opinion that the village owes its existence to the Banas mentioned above as descendants of the demon Maha Bali (or Mahabali Chakravarthi). But in ancient Cola inscriptions found at the Seven Pagodas, the name of the place is Mamallapuram, which is evidently a corruption of Mahamallapuram, meaning the city or town of Mamalla. I have already mentioned the fact that Mahamalla occurs as a surname of the Pallava King Narasimha Varman I. in a mutilated record at Badami (an ancient Pallava stronghold) in the Bombay Presidency. It is thus not unlikely that Mahamallapuram or Mavalavaram was founded by the Pallava King Narasimha Varman, the contemporary and opponent of the Calukya Pulikesan II., whose accession took place about A.D. 609. Professor Hultzsch is of opinion that the earliest inscriptions on the Rathas are Virudus of a King named Narasimha. It may therefore be concluded that the village was originally called Mahamallapuram or Mamallapuram, after the Pallava King Narasimha Varman I., and that the earliest of the Rathas were cut out by him. The remaining Rathas must also have come into existence during the period of Pallava supremacy, but perhaps at a somewhat later date."

Vincent Smith ("History of Fine Art in India and Ceylon, 1911") follows Venkayya, and states that the correct name of the place is Mamallapuram, "the town of Mamalla" or Narasimha Varman I., and that the forms Mahabalipur, Mavallipur, etc., in common use are corruptions based on a false etymology.

II.—CHARACTER OF THE INSCRIPTIONS

The inscriptions at the Seven Pagodas have been published in Dr. Hultzsch's "South Indian Inscriptions," vol. i. As regards the Sanscrit inscriptions, Dr. Hultzsch states that four different alphabets are employed in the Pallava inscriptions of Mamallapuram and Salavankuppam (two miles north of the former). The first very archaic alphabet is found in all but one of the inscriptions of the so-called Dharmaraja Rath. The bulk of the Mamallapuram inscriptions—viz., those of the so-called Ganesa temple, Dharmaraja Mantapam and Ramanuja Mantapam—with one of the inscriptions of the Dharmaraja Ratha are written in the second, an extremely florid character. The third alphabet occurs on the northern, and the fourth on the southern, wall of the Atiranachandesvara temple at Salvankuppam. Dr. Burnell assigns the first alphabet to about the fifth century, the second to about A.D. 700, the third to the eighth or ninth century, and the fourth to the eleventh century, A.D. To this I have only to add that the second alphabet probably belongs to the sixth century, as it resembles that of Rajasimha's and Mahendravarman's inscriptions at Kanchipuram.

The most important inscriptions, in the form of slokas, are to be found in the last of the five Rathas to the south, and in the Ganesa temple on the ridge-shaped hill, containing the bas-reliefs and caves. The only fact set forth in these inscriptions is that a certain King Jayaram (known also by the epithet Kamaraja) erected to Siva the shrine in question. The language being Sanscrit is a clear proof of their Brahminical or northern origin. Previous to the seventh century A.D., the whole of the district in which Mamallapur stands was occupied by the Kurumbas (or Pallavas as they styled themselves later on), a half-civilised people of the Jain religion, and it was about that period, or later, that the Brahmans were introduced into this part of the country by the Chola King Adondai, whose capitals were at Conjeeveram and Tirupathi.

The oldest of the Tamil inscriptions is cut on a niche on the face of the rock on which the modern Vishnu temple is dedicated to Varahaswami (the Boar incarnation). They commemorate gifts of land made by inhabitants of the locality. The Tamil characters are simple, and therefore the language is of some antiquity, and must have been written about the eleventh century.

III.—THE PALLAVAS

The following notes are compiled from Mr. Venkayya's article in the Archæological Report for 1906-1907, and Sewell's antiquities :

"The word Pallava is apparently the Sanscrit form of the tribal name Pahlava or Pahnava of the Puranas. The Pahlavas are described as a northern or north-western tribe, whose territory lay somewhere between the River Indus and Persia. They are said to be Kshatriyas originally, but became degraded in later times. The word Pahlava is believed to be a corruption of Parthava or Parthia, and Dr. Bhandarkar calls the Indo-Parthians, Pahlavas. The Pahlavas of the east coast (who finally settled in Kanchipuram) were the political successors of the Andhras in the Telugu country, when they ceased to be the ruling power in the third century; they moved into Godaveri and Kistna deltas about the middle of the second century. They therefore must have come from Persia."

The Pallavas became the possessors of an extensive kingdom lying mostly along the east coast of the Peninsula, but at one period extending apparently over almost the whole of the Deccan. Their capital in Southern India was Kanchi or Conjeeveram. As usual with the other kingdoms of ancient India, their possessions greatly varied at different periods, but they seem to have been one of the principal southern Powers when first the Chalukyas emigrated from Northern India about the fifth century A.D. Early in the seventh century, the Pallavas were driven out of their northern possessions by the first of the eastern Chalukyan dynasty, and about the same time Pulikesin II. of the Western Chalukyas of Badami states that he drove the Pallava Sovereign behind the walls of Kanchi. His successor, Vikramaditya I. (A.D. 652-680), was, it seems, conquered by the Pallavas, but towards the third quarter of the eighth century Nandhivarman was defeated by Vikramaditya II., and is believed to be the last King of the Pallava family. The Pallavas appear to have been Saivas at first, and accordingly adopted the bull for their crest and the club for their banner. Some of the Kings were probably adherents of the Vaishnava faith. In A.D. 640 Hiven-Thsang visited Kanchi as the capital of the kingdom of Dravida, which he describes. The Jains, who believe that penance is necessary to salvation and that even inorganic matter has a soul, were very numerous in his day; Buddhists and Brahminical worshippers were about equal in strength. About this period (A.D. 600-700) flourished the great Siva reformer

Sankaracharyar, who is said to have preached at Kanchi.

In 788 the Buddhists were finally expelled from the neighbourhood of Kanchi to Ceylon. In the eleventh century the power of the Pallavas was crushed by the Cholas, and Kanchi then became the capital of the Chola Province called Thondaimandalam. (About this time Ramanuja Chariar was born at Sriperumbudur, about fifteen miles from Conjeeveram, and converted many to the Vaishnava faith.)

Tondaiyar appears to have been the name of the Pallavas, according to Tamil literature, and the Pallava King was called Tondaiman. The origin of the name is obscure. Tradition has it that the first Tondaiman was the illegitimate son of a Chola King and a Naga woman. It has also been suggested that the original name of the province bestowed on this illegitimate Chola province was Tondaimandalam, *i.e.*—the province of slaves.

There are some very old temples in Siva Kanchi, or Big Conjeeveram. Two dedicated to Siva are very much alike, and are exceedingly interesting as being probably types of the structures from which the cave-diggers of the Seven Pagodas drew their designs.

There is a large Vishnu temple dedicated to Vaikunta Perumal, and built by Paramesvara-varman II., son of Rajasimha. The characteristic of the Gopura is that, though composed of all the members used, it is really not so much a Gopura as a series of stories or terraces, one above the other, each smaller than the one below, and surmounted by a Khalasa. In this tower we have the link between the old Vihara and the more modern Gopura. It is not a tower at all, but consists of a series of stories with the edges of the platforms guarded by low walls in which are imitation cells. Later on this form grew into a tower with imitation platforms, and the cells became mere ornaments on the tower wall. The Kailasanatha temple built by the Pallava King Rajsimha is the most interesting, and perhaps the oldest, at Conjeeveram. There are sculptures here not unlike those of the Seven Pagodas.

We have now to examine if there are any Pallavas in our midst beyond the royal family of Pudukkottai. The Pallavas are believed to be identical with the Kurumbars, of whom the Kurumbar of the Tamil country and the Kurumbars of the Canarese districts and of the Mysore State may be taken as the living representatives.

The Pallavas seemed to have settled down as cultivators soon after all traces of their sovereignty disappeared.

The following note is from Howells's "The Soul of India," pp. 187 and 188: "The origin of the Pallava clan or tribe is obscure. The name, however, is identical with Pallava, and ultimately with Parthiva or Parthian. They must have come originally from the countries beyond the north-western frontier of India, about the beginning of the Christian era, and gradually worked their way down to Malabar and the Coromandel coast. In the second century A.D. they are classed in native writers with the Sakas and Yavanas, the objects of hostility to native Kings. They do not seem to have actually colonised and directly administered much territory of their own, but, like the Marathas in later times, they appear to have imposed tribute on the territorial Governments of the country. The three principalities of Kanchi, Vengi, and Palakkadu (in Malabar) were, however, known as the three Pallava dominions, Kanchi being regarded as the headquarters of the clan. Three of the eleven Kings of the south conquered by Samudragupta in the fourth century were Pallavas. The visit of the Chinese pilgrim to Kanchi in 640 A.D., and the temporary overthrow of the Chalukya power by the Pallava monarch two years later, have already been referred to. The conflict between the Chalukyas and Pallavas became perennial, and the successors of the Chalukyas—viz., the Rashtrakutas—took up the old quarrel with the Pallavas. Rajaraja the Great, the victorious Chola monarch, towards the end of the tenth century, destroyed the Pallava power, which had lasted for nearly ten centuries. The later Pallava chiefs were feudatory nobles and officials in the service of the territorial kingdoms. The Raja of the Pudukottai Tributary State styles himself Raja Pallava, and claims descent from the ancient royal family. The Pallava Kings were generally orthodox Hindus, though one was a Buddhist. Several were devoted to the cult of Vishnu, but in later times they became inclined to the Siva cult.

Mr. S. Krishnaswami Aiyengar refers to the Pallavas in the following lines:

"In the reign of Duttagamani, King of Ceylon (101-77 B.C.), a vast assembly of Bhikkus were called together from various Buddhist centres. Among them we find mention of a place called

Pallavabogga, placed in the narrative between Kasmira and Alasanda, the city of Yonas. Immediately after this comes the monastery by the road of the Vindhya forest mountains. Professor Greiger seems inclined to locate this Alasanda in the Paroponisus or the Hindukush, but we have to look for it rather on this side of the mountains into India. Bearing in mind that it is not safe to infer from the order of statement the geographical location of places, it will still stand to reason to locate this somewhere about Sind, in which reign there were Alexandrias enough, Karachi itself being among them, and Kandahar. The placing of the Pallavabogga in this locality is in keeping with the fact that about A.D. 130 the Andra King Gotamiputra claims to have defeated the Pallavas, along with Sakas and Yavanas. A little later, about A.D. 150, Rudhradhaman had a Pallava Minister Suvisaka, according to the Junagadh inscription of Rudhradhaman. It was from this position that they were moving gradually south-eastwards, till at the time of the break of the Andra power they are found in the reign of Guntur. When in the Deccan the power of the Andras went to pieces about the middle of the third century A.D., these found themselves the heirs of the eastern part as the Chalukyas became heirs of the western. Of these two the Pallavas seem to have made good their position earlier, so that Samudra Gupta, in the course of his conquest, found them a well-settled power on his borders, Yuvamaharaja Vishnugopa of Kanchi figuring in his Allahabad Pillar inscription of about A.D. 350, while there is no mention of the Chalukyas at all. With this ruler the Pallavas came into a prominence which they maintained unbroken for a period of about four centuries, when they split up into a number of principalities which got easily swallowed up in the rising empire of the Cholas. This period of Pallava ascendancy is one of very great importance in the history of India.

IV.—THE CHALUKYAS

The Chalukyas came originally from the north, and from the sixth to the twelfth century they maintained a sovereignty extremely powerful though sometimes nominal. The descent of the Kings is traced in the Lunar Race through a succession of fifty-nine sovereigns ruling in Ayodhya to one Vijayaditya, who journeyed southwards bent on conquest, but who lost his life in battle. His son, Vishnu Vardhana, made extensive conquests, strengthening his authority by an alliance with the Pallava King of Kanchi, whose daughter he married. The grandsons of Pulikesan I. (grandson of Vishnu Vardhana) separated and became the ancestors of the western and eastern Chalukyas, the elder remaining in the Western Deccan, while the younger Kubja Vishnuvardhana obtained possession of the eastern coast by conquering the Kings of Vengi (Pallavas). The conquest was a triumph of the Brahminical religion over Buddhism. The Vengi Kings were Buddhists, and they seem to have succeeded the Buddhist Andra on the Krishna River, while the Chalukyas were Vaishnavas. Satyastaya or Pulikesi II. was one of the most powerful princes of the Western Chalukyas. He drove the Pallavas behind the walls of Kanchi and prepared to conquer the Cholas with a large army. Hiwen Thsang gives an interesting account of his kingdom. Presents and letters were interchanged between him and Khosru II., contemporary King of Persia. It is certain that the Cholas were conquered by the Chalukyas shortly before the beginning of the eleventh century. The power of the Kalachuri and Ganapati Kings and the rise of the Hoysala Ballala dynasty of Mysore decided the fate of the western Chalukyas, and they disappear after 1189. The Ganapati sovereigns acquired power also in the eastern Chalukyan territories, and they finally ejected the Chola Chalukyas about the year 1228.

V.—THE HINDU GODS

The Vedas—four in number—are the earliest religious books of the Hindus. They are not the work of one man, but according to popular belief were communicated to certain Rishis or Saints. Each of the Vedas are divided into two parts—hymns and ritualistic precept. In the latter are found instructions to the priests who conduct the worship of the Gods addressed in the hymns. The Vedic Gods are three—Agni (fire) in earth, Indra (rain) in air, and Suyra (sun) in heaven. Each of these has various appellations according to differences of function giving rise to the three orders of deities allied in sphere and functions. The Vedas are the special property of the Brahmans, and in the code of Manu, compiled about two or three centuries later than the Vedas and which divides the Hindus into four castes, it was regarded as an offence for a single word of the divinely given books to be heard by a man of a lower caste.

The Arya Samajists, a reformed body, accept the inspiration of the hymn of the Vedas only, while the Brahmo-Samajists reject entirely the Vedas as inspired scriptures.

VI.–MODERN HINDU RELIGION

The modern mythology of the Hindus are in the two great epics—the Ramayana (about 500 B.C.) and the Mahabaratha, in the Puranas—which are traditional stories, and the Tantras which are in the form of a dialogue between Siva and his wife. These books may be read by other than Brahmans.

According to modern Hindu religion, which is a development of Brahminism, the Puranic deities are three in number.

The esoteric doctrine is that there is one God with many manifestations, which may be taken either as representing a portion of his divinity, his appearance for a specific purpose, or as symbols of his different powers.

Brahma is regarded as the Supreme Being, the God of Gods, of whom Brahma, Vishnu, and Siva are manifestations.

BRAHMA

Brahma, the first of the triad, is called the Creator. He is represented with four faces and four arms, and his symbols are a portion of the Veda, a spoon, a rosary, and a vessel of lustral water.

Brahma's wife is Sarasvathi, the Goddess of wisdom and science, the mother of the Vedas and the inventor of the Devanagari letters. She is represented seated on a white lotus playing a kind of Banjo.

VISHNU

Vishnu is the second person of the Hindu triad. In pictures he is represented as a black man with four arms ; in one hand he holds a club, in another a shell, in the third a Chakra, or discus, with which he slew his enemies, and in the fourth a lotus. He rides upon the bird Garuda (eagle).

Lakshmi is the wife of Vishnu. She is regarded as the Goddess of Love, Beauty, and Prosperity, and she is represented as seated on a red lotus.

PANEL OF BRAHMA IN THE TRIMURTHI CAVE (page 76).

Narayana is a name of Vishnu, specially considered as the deity who was before all worlds, whose resting-place (Ayana) was on the primeval waters (Nara).

Hindu mythology applies the terms sometimes to Brahma and also to Siva, but when applied to Vishnu it is in the act of willing creation. Under this character he is represented as lying on the lotus as well as on the thousand-headed serpent Sesha.

Serpent Worship connected with Vishnu

There are some people to this day who are devoted to serpent worship and who will not kill a cobra even near a dwelling-house, because they look upon it as the guardian deity of the place. Under the dense perennial foliage of a Pipal-tree (*Ficus religiosa*) may be seen erected slabs of granite with snakes intertwining themselves engraved on them and before which devotees prostrate themselves. When it is acknowledged that the immortal soul may dwell in any form of life it is not difficult to believe that the deity in some aspect or other may not be most properly represented by animal forms. The serpent-god is a good illustration of this belief. Talboys Wheeler observes that the doctrine of transmigration appears to have grown out of the mysteries of death and reproduction which were associated with the worship of the serpent and the Linga. As an ancient faith in the south it seems to have been overthrown about the eighth century by Buddhism, and the bas-relief of Arjuna's penance commemorates the attempt to engraft the tolerant religion of the Quietists on the faith of a nation of worshippers of the Great Serpent God.

Balarama is an incarnation of the Serpent Adhisesha, who himself is part of Vishnu, and thus is said to be a part of that deity.

Sesha, the Serpent Deity, has a thousand heads, and forms the couch on which Vishnu reposes, during intervals of creation. The Hindus believe that at the end of every creation all things are absorbed into the deity, and in the interval of another creation he reposeth himself upon the Serpent Sesha (duration). In popular language, the world is said to rest on the head of Sesha, who stands upon a tortoise; when therefore the tortoise moves his feet, or Sesha yawns, earthquakes result. It was this serpent that formed the rope at the churning of the ocean, and by fires that issue from his body the world is destroyed at the end of each age or Kalpa.

The Incarnations or Avataras of Vishnu

I. Mathsaya or Fish Avatara

The Lord of the Universe assumes many bodily shapes. The first was that of a fish. In this form Vishnu entered into the ocean to fight with the Asuras who made away with the Vedas, and thus delivered them from their hands.

2. The Kurma or Tortoise Avatara

This incarnation was necessitated by the fact that the Gods were in danger of losing their authority over the demons. In their distress they applied to Vishnu for help, who told them to churn the sea of milk, that they might procure the Amrita or water of life by which they would be made strong, promising to become the tortoise on which the mountain Mandara as a churning-stick should rest.

3. VARAHA (BOAR) AVATARA

The object was to raise the earth from the ocean in which it was submerged by a demon Hiranyaksha. The form of a boar was chosen because it was the animal delighting in water, and just the animal to bore the earth and uplift it by its tusks. It is also regarded as a type of the ritual of the Vedas, for which reason the elevation of the earth on the tusks of a boar is regarded as an allegorical representation of the extrication of the world from a deluge of sin by the rites of religion.

4. NARASIMHA OR (MAN-LION) AVATARA

The demon Hiranyaksha had a brother named Hiranya-Kasipu, who had obtained a boon from Brahma that he should not be slain by any created being. When, therefore, his pride, fostered by his supposed immunity from danger, had led him to great excesses, so that his death was desired both by Gods and men, Vishnu descended in the form of a living being, half man and half lion, and slew him.

5. THE VAMANA OR (DWARF) AVATARA

This incarnation was undertaken to recover heaven for the Gods. Bali, a demon, was King over the three worlds—heaven, earth, and the netherworld. In the form of a Brahman dwarf Vishnu appears, and asks as a gift as much land as he could cross over in three steps. This the King grants. Immediately the pigmy assumes a gigantic growth, and with two steps strides over heaven and earth, and with the third placed on Bali's head crushes him to death, and the latter then obtains salvation.

6. THE PARASURAMA AVATARA

The incarnation of Parasurama or Rama with axe was undertaken by Vishnu for the purpose of exterminating the Kshatriya or warrior caste, which had tried to assert its authority over the Brahminical.

7. THE RAMACHANDRA AVATARA

In Northern India this is perhaps the most popular of all the incarnations of Vishnu, and the Ramayana in which his history is found contains some of the most beautiful legends in the whole of the sacred writings of the Hindus. The great exploit and main subject of the epic is the war which Rama waged with the giant Ravana, the fierce and mighty King of Lunka or Ceylon. Thus he became not only the benefactor of the Gods, but their saviour and friend, and he slew their enemy, Ravana.

8. KRISHNA AND BALARAMA AVATARA

The two brothers, Krishna and Balarama, form the eighth incarnation, Krishna having been produced from a black and Balarama from a white heir of Vishnu. Evil spirits had begun to commit great crimes in the world, and Vishnu, when appealed to by the distressed Gods to appear on earth to save them from their oppressors, became incarnate. The legends connected with them give us an opportunity to trace the Hindu antiquity, the gradual transformation of mortal heroes into representatives of a God.

9. THE BUDDHA AVATARA

This is alluded to in some of the Puranas, the intention being to effect a compromise between

Brahminism and Buddhism by trying to represent the latter religion as not irreconcilably antagonistic to the former.

10. THE KALKI AVATARA

This incarnation has yet to be made. It is the hope of the Hindus that he who has so frequently visited the earth to restore order and happiness will come yet again to inaugurate a reign of universal goodness, peace, and prosperity.

The first four Avataras occurred in the age of truth, the Golden Age, the Kritha Yuga, when castes were alike in their functions.

The second Yuga is the Tretha. In this age sacrifice commenced and righteousness decreased by a quarter. In the Dwapara Yuga righteousness was diminished by two-fourths and the Vedas became fourfold. The scriptures being thus divided, ceremonies were celebrated in a great variety of ways.

In the Kali Yuga righteousness remained to the extent of one-quarter. It is an age of strife and dissension. At its termination Vishnu is expected to come again and establish a kingdom of righteousness similar to the first Yuga. These four ages will, in the same order and with similar characteristics, again and again appear until the final end of all things shall come.

The various incarnations of Vishnu reveal an inner philosophical truth besides the apparent meaning suggested by the different bodily shapes assumed by him for different purposes. They all represent the successive stages of evolution, and have an analogous bearing to Darwin's theory of evolution.

SIVA

Siva is the third person of the Hindu triad. As Brahma was creator, Vishnu preserver, in order to complete the system as all things are subject to decay, a destroyer was necessary, and destruction is regarded as the peculiar work of Siva. But in the Hindu sense he who destroys causes beings to assume new phases of existence—the destroyer being really a re-creator.

The ordinary name by which Siva in known is Mahadeva, the great God. He is also known as Eswara, and is represented with four arms. His symbols are the trident, a noose, an antelope, and a drum. Each God is represented as having special fondness for some bird or animal on which he is supposed to travel, and which therefore is called his Vahan or vehicle. The bull is Siva's. Vishnu rides on an eagle, Brahma has the goose, and Ganesa the rat.

The consort of Siva is Parvati, represented in pictures as a beautiful but ordinary woman. It is when she appears as Durga or Kali that she manifests divine powers for the destruction of demons.

The son of Siva is called Kartikeya, because he was nursed by the Kritikas, the personified Pleiades, and in South India he is known as Subrahmaniya, because he is the special guardian of the Brahminical order. He rides on the peacock.

The Worship of the Lingam in connection with Siva

Though Siva is usually represented in the human form, it is in the form of the Linga that he is almost universally worshipped. This image does not suggest anything offensive to the Hindu, who believes the emblem to be symbolic of the attributes ascribed to him by his worshippers as the Supreme Lord, the beginning of all existences, the Cause of Causes.

GANESA

Parvati, the wife of Siva, was having a bath in her lord's absence, and to secure privacy fashioned Ganesa from the turmeric paste with which she had anointed her body, and set him down at the door to keep off intruders. Siva returning found the way barred, and in a rage cut off his head. Parvati would not be satisfied until Siva had promised to restore Ganesa to life. The latter's head could not be found, so Siva went off into the forest and found an elephant sleeping with his head turned towards the north. He cut off this head and fitted it on to Ganesa.

Allegory.—Ganesa is the protector of households, represents the wisdom which brings to mankind a great store of this world's goods. He was not born of the perfect union of the soul and matter, Purusha and Prakirthi, but was fashioned from the dross of mother earth, and his vehicle is the mean earth-burrowing creature, the rat.

DRAUPADI

She is the common wife of the five Pandava brothers. Drupada, King of Panchala, held a Swayamvara (a tournament in which his daughter

Draupadi chose for herself a husband), at which Arjuna displayed great skill in the use of the bow by piercing a fish that was suspended in the air without looking directly at the object; he saw its image only reflected in a pan of water on the ground. Arjuna having been selected was returning home with his brothers. He then saw his mother and told her that he had brought home a "kanni" (girl), and invited her opinion as to what she wished him to do with the same. The mother, who thought she heard him say "kani," meaning a fruit, wished him to divide it equally among the five brothers. The word of a mother could not be set aside, and thus Draupadi became the wife of each.

The following is taken from the Iconographical notes on the Seven Pagodas by Dr. J. Pl. Vogel, which appear in the Annual Report, 1910-11, of the Archæological Survey of India:

Dharmaraja's Ratha

Popular tradition connects it with the name of Dharmaraja (King of the sacred Law). This temple is provided with three tiers of niches containing figures of deities. In the lowermost row, which decorates the body of the temple, there are two figures on each side, making altogether eight figures, which are nearly all two-armed, and appear to belong to the Saiva Pantheon. Among them we notice on the back (east side) a four-armed figure of Siva Ardhanarisa, his right half being male and the left female. It is one of those curious creations of the Indian mind which are due rather to phantasy than to good taste. The upper right hand holds a hatchet, the upper left an indistinct object. The other two hands are empty, the right one being raised in the gesture of imparting protection (*abhaya*). It will be noticed that a cobra serves as a girdle.

The central and upper tiers of image niches decorate the roof. In the central row we have on the south side seven figures. The deep niche in the centre enshrines a standing Vishnu figure, with high tiara, which has four arms and holds a wheel in the upper right and a conch in the upper left hand.

The adjoining shallow panel to the proper right contains a four-armed God leaning on a male attendant, slightly stooping. A similar group is found on the north wall of Arjuna's Rath.

The corresponding shallow panel to the proper

left contains a four-armed male leaning on a dwarf and holding a staff (or perhaps a flute) in both hands. The other right hand holds an indistinct object, perhaps a thunderbolt. The second left hand is placed on the head of the attending dwarf.

The next panel to the proper right shows a two-armed male defeating a three-hooded Naga, whose snake tail he holds with both hands. Both figures are two-armed. The group possibly represents Krishna vanquishing the Kaliya Naga.

The corresponding figure to the upper left is a four-armed Siva, who holds a cobra and a trident in his left upper and lower hands respectively, and a hatchet in his right upper. The other right hand is broken. He wears a high head-dress with crescent and skull. A male figure is prostrated at his feet.

In the panel on the upper right end there is a four-armed male deity holding a sword in one of his right hands. The other emblems are uncertain. One of his left hands rests on his hip.

On the proper left end we have a four-armed figure who carries a rosary (*akshamala* shown standing up !) in his right upper hand and a fly-whisk (*Chamara*) in his left upper hand. The other left hand is placed on his hip. The object in his second right hand is irrecognizable.

On the north wall the deeply carved central panel contains a four-armed standing figure of Vishnu holding in his upper right hand a wheel whereas on his left he carries a kneeling femaes figure worshipping him. The two remaining hands are held in front of his breast.

Adjoining the central panel to the proper right we notice again that curious group found on the south side and also on Arjuna's Rath (north side). The present relief is slightly different. The main figure is evidently Vishnu, as appears from his high tiara and the emblems—the wheel (*chakra*) and the conch shell (*sankha*)—in his upper right and left hands respectively. The other left hand rests on the shoulder of the attendant, who is stooping, and presses two fingers of his right hand on his lips, the left being placed on his knee. Is this posture meant to indicate that he is panting under the weight of the deity whom he is supporting?

The next figure to the proper right is a four-armed Siva, with a skull in his braided hair-tuft (*Jata*), dancing over a defeated demon.

On the proper right end we find Siva again

Panel of Siva and Parvati in Second Storey of Dharmaraja's Ratha (page 91).

(page 91)

leaning on his vehicle the bull. He is four-armed. In his upper right and left hands he holds a damaram and a rosary (*akshamala*) or noose (*pasa*). The other two hands are empty; the right rests on the bull.

The shallow panel adjoining the central one on the proper left contains two male figures. The main personage is four-armed, and stands with a bow in one of his left hands, the other left hand being placed on the shoulder of his attendant. The bow suggests Rama, but is he ever figured with four arms? If so, the attendant would probably be his brother Lakshmana.

The next figure, which is placed in a deep panel, is again Siva with four arms, two of which hold a hatchet or battle-axe to the right and a trident (*trisula*) to the left. He is accompanied by a male attendant.

In the top row we find on the west side—that is, in the façade—a chapel or cell with a relief carved on its back wall. This sculpture represents the well-known group (the "Siva at home" tableau) of Siva and Parvathi peculiar to Pallava art. The four-armed Siva distinguished by the crescent in his head-dress (*Chandra Sekhara*) is seated to front on a bench, with Parvathi turned towards him on his left side. She is two-armed and holds a child, presumably Karttikeya, on her knee. In the upper corners we notice the usual flying dwarfs, probably *Ganas*, apparently waving fly-whisks. There is a four-armed attendant on each side of the main group. In front of the group there is a square mortice indicating the place of the Linga, which must have formed the object of worship in this shrine. There is an outlet for sacrificial water to the north. On either side of the entrance to the chapel there are two *Dwarapalas*; all four are two-armed, those to the proper right holding a mace and a flower.

Arjuna's Ratha

The central niche on the back wall of Arjuna's Ratha shows a figure mounted on an elephant facing. It is supposed to represent the thunder-god, Indra, who was Arjuna's divine father. That the figure actually is meant for Indra is not at all improbable, if we may judge from his vehicle. The remaining figures on Arjuna's Rath do not offer anything remarkable.

INTERIOR PANEL FROM DRAUPADI RATHA (page 93).

Draupadi's Ratha

The back wall is carved with a relief representing a four-armed goddess standing on a lotus. Fergusson assumes that she represents Lakshmi; but it will be seen later on that there is good reason to identify her as Durga or Parvathi. At her feet are two kneeling figures, probably of donors. The one to the proper right is a male, who with his left hand grasps his tuft (*chuda*) of hair, which apparently he is in the act of cutting with a sword held in his right hand. The attitude of this figure is very striking. Can the figures in this attitude refer to a hair-offering, a well-known practice of various ancient nations?

It is clear that the popular designations of the five so-called Raths is purely phantastical. All over India ancient buildings are connected with the five Pandava brothers and their common spouse, Draupadi.

The only temple regarding the real origin of which a definite statement can be made is Dharmaraja; for it is recorded in two inscriptions found on the building that it was "the Isvara (Siva) temple of Atyantakama Pallava." Atyantakama, according to Dr. Hultzsch, is the same as the Pallava King Narasimha Varman I., surnamed Mahamalla, who reigned in the first half of the seventh century, and who gave his name to Mamalla (that is, Mahamalla) puram. That the temple was dedicated to Siva appears also from the relief in the cella, and from the fact that this cella must once have contained a *Linga*. For a tentative identification of two of the remaining four temples it is important to note that among the group we find three life-size animals cut out of the same rock. They are placed at random, but I have little doubt that they were intended to be finally placed in front of the respective shrines to which they belong.

The bull was probably intended to be placed in front of the Dharmaraja, which, as we saw, is in reality a Siva temple. The lion had not to be shifted very far to come right opposite the entrance of the Devi (popularly Draupadi) temple. If this was indeed the intention of the sculptures, it would follow that the goddess depicted in the relief inside the temple represents Durga or Parvati. This assumption would well agree with the circumstance that the niche in the back wall contains a figure of the demon-slaying goddess.

THE RATHAS WITH ELEPHANT AND LION CARVED IN STONE (page 94).

The elephant is the vehicle of Indra, and we may therefore assume that the so-called Rath of Arjuna was in reality a shrine dedicated to Indra, whose effigy we have, moreover, recognized in the centre of the back wall.

The Mahishasura Mantapa

The so-called Mahishasura Mantapa is, in reality, a cave-temple dedicated to Siva. This is evident from the relief carved on the back wall of the cella. It is very similar to that found in the Linga shrine of the so-called Dharmaraja Rath, of which a description has been given above. Here also we have a four-armed Siva with a high tiara and halo, seated to front, and at his left side Parvati holding a child, presumably Karttikeya, on her knee. Over the head of the goddess there are traces of a parasol. We notice two more figures in the background behind Siva. They are four-armed, and must represent Brahma and Vishnu, the two other members of the Hindu Trinity. The former holds a water-pot (*kamandalu*) and a lotus-flower ; the latter has his usual emblems, the wheel (*chakra*) and the conch (*sankha*). Beneath is Siva's vehicle, the bull

Nandhi lying at his feet. Besides, there is a small female figure at the feet of Parvati. The two lions on both sides indicate the throne, or *simbasana.* The back wall contains two side-chapels, in which originally *Lingas* must have been placed.

The temple has received its popular designation from one of the two large reliefs carved on the side walls. This relief, which is found on the right-hand wall on entering, represents Durga defeating Mahishasura.

The slaying of the Buffalo Demon by Durga is a very favourite subject, not only in India proper, but also in Java.

On the opposite wall we find another familiar scene—namely, the sleep of Vishnu.

At the lower end of Vishnu's couch are two colossal figures standing in an attitude of defiance, the one in front holding a mace. They may be identified with Madhu and Kaitabha, the two demons who sprang up from Vishnu's ear-secretion during his sleep. Over the sleeping god we notice two flying figures, of which the second has the appearance of a goblin or *gana.* The other, perhaps, represents the goddess Yoganidra-Dura, born from the wrath

PANEL OF KALI IN THE TIRUMURTHI CAVE (page 97).

of the gods for the destruction of the evil spirits.

If this identification is correct, it would follow that the present sculpture also relates to the legend of the goddess Durga, like that on the opposite wall.

The Varaha Avatara

The female figure is the Earth saved by Vishnu from the abyss ; and the demon trodden under foot must be the Daitya Hiranyaksha—" Gold Eye "—here shown in the shape of a Naga.

The Trimurthi Mandapa

The so-called Trimurthi Mandapa is a cave-temple near the " Gopi's Churn." It contains three cells. The central one has a relief carved on the back wall representing Siva standing, four-armed. In his upper right hand he holds the wheel, in his upper left the conch (broken), while the other two hands are empty. In the proper right cell is a figure of Brahma standing, four-armed.

Arjuna's Penance

There is some reason to assume that this designation has as little connection with the original meaning of this gigantic sculpture as the popular names of the so-called Raths. It is true that among the numerous figures rather a prominent place is taken by an ascetic standing on one leg and stretching his two arms upwards (*Urdhva-bahu*) in the position so often described in the old Indian epics. But there is nothing to indicate that this figure represents Arjuna.

Fergusson assumed that the free standing figures of a Naga and a Nagi, which occupy their places, one above the other, inside the cleft itself, were the real objects of adoration, and that, therefore, the whole scene relates to Naga worship. But it has been rightly pointed out that this interpretation is impossible, as the two Naga figures themselves assume the same attitude of namaskara as the other demi-gods, Gandarvas and Apsaras, Kinnaras and Kinnaris, and so on. There are, moreover, a Naga and Nagi among the figures approaching the fissure from the proper right.

Dr. Marshall has suggested that possibly there has once been a detached image (perhaps of Buddha or a lingam) standing in front of the rock and forming the real object of worship. But excavation carried out on the spot has revealed no trace of such a figure.

Can it be that once there existed here a sacred spring and that the water gushing forth from the cleft was the real aim and object of all the adoring figures? The presence of the Nagas would then be most easily accounted for, as they are the water-spirits dwelling in lakes and springs.

A geologist may perhaps be able to decide whether the former existence of a spring of fresh water on this spot is at all possible or probable.

VII.—GENERAL REMARKS ON THE SCULPTURES

A striking characteristic of the sculptures is their sober and moderate style, in which they contrast strongly with the productions of the medieval plastic art of India. Here we do not find the exaggeration of form, the exuberance of ornament, and the want of proportion which disfigure those later sculptures.

It will be noticed that the majority of the deities represented are either two or four armed. The only exceptions are the Vishnu in the scene of the Vamana Avatara, the goddess in the Trimurthi cave, and the goddess Durga defeating the demon king.

We know that in later sculpture Vishnu is invariably four-armed (*Chatur-buja*), and that his attributes are the wheel (*chakra*), the lotus (*Padma*), and the mace (*gada*). It would seem, however, that in the seventh century neither the number of his arms nor his attributes were finally fixed. It is true that the Vishnu images of Mamallapuram are usually four-armed—*e.g.*, the two noticed among the figures on the Dharmaraja and the one in Trimurthi cave. But in this respect they do not differ from the effigies of other deities. It is also remarkable that in the instances quoted there are only two emblems, namely, the conch and the wheel held in the upper pair of hands, whereas the other pair is empty. It is evident, therefore, that the extra pair was not added, as might have been expected, in order to make it possible to provide the figure with two more attributes. The real object of the sculpture was apparently to bring out the divine nature of the personage represented by giving him a superhuman shape.

Most of the four-armed figures of deities found here are only provided with two emblems, the other two hands being empty. Of the latter the left usually rests on the hip, and the right is raised in the attitude indicating the imparting of protection. It deserves notice that the two emblems, the wheel and the conch, are not particular to Vishnu exclusively, for we saw that the goddess Durga seems to be portrayed with the same attributes.

Another point of interest is that the deities figured in these carvings are not provided with haloes. There are only a few exceptions to this rule. In the so-called "Penance of Arjuna" we find two figures with circular haloes hovering on both sides of what is generally supposed to be the central group of this rock-sculpture. These two haloed figures have been explained as Surya and Chandra. This explanation is probably correct, and when we meet with other instances of figures with haloes, we may perhaps assume that they represent one or both of these deities.

Note.—Most of the illustrations are from photographs supplied by the Archæological Survey Department, Madras.

INDEX